PRAISE FOR *RUNAGATE*

"Crystal Simone Smith's poetry sparkles with clarity—haiku allows nothing less. She offers searing attention to the wounds of the past. The imagery and formal look of each poem on the page also reveal her gifts as a visual artist. Here are poems our ancestors deserve."—TSITSI ELLA JAJI, author of *Mother Tongues: Poems*

"The voices of the self-liberating African Americans that Crystal Simone Smith reclaims in *Runagate* are resolutely alive. Smith captures the emotive and embodying possibilities of haiku and tanka to invite readers to reckon with their rejection of 'the laws of slavery' and invite us to imagine their lives beyond the confines of the posters and capture notices that once held their histories. This is the poetry of destiny, revealing Smith's grasp of the infinite possibilities of formal poetics and of the living spirits who dared to claim freedom for themselves, and for those of us who are blessed to hear their stories."—SHEILA SMITH MCKOY, author of *The Bones Beneath*

RUNAGATE

RUNAGATE

§ SONGS *of* THE FREEDOM BOUND §

Crystal Simone Smith

DUKE UNIVERSITY PRESS *Durham and London* 2025

Project Editor: Lisa Lawley

Designed by Matthew Tauch

Typeset in Adobe Jenson Pro, Chaparral Pro, and
ITC Frankin Gothic Std by Copperline Book Services

Library of Congress Cataloging-in-Publication Data
Names: Smith, Crystal Simone, author.
Title: Runagate : songs of the freedom bound / Crystal Simone Smith.
Description: Durham : Duke University Press, 2025.
Identifiers: LCCN 2024041567 (print)
LCCN 2024041568 (ebook)
ISBN 9781478031819 (paperback)
ISBN 9781478028581 (hardcover)
ISBN 9781478060796 (ebook)
Subjects: LCSH: Slave narratives—Poetry. | Enslaved persons— Poetry.
| Slavery—Poetry. | LCGFT: Haiku. | Tanka. | Poetry. Classification: LCC
PS3619.M5739 R86 2025 (print) |
LCC PS3619.M5739 (ebook) | DDC 811.008/352625—dc23/eng/20241120
LC record available at https://lccn.loc.gov/2024041567
LC ebook record available at https://lccn.loc.gov/2024041568

Cover art: Paul Evans, *Moonlight Stroll*, 2020. Courtesy
of the artist.

—FOR MY MANY GREAT-GRANDPARENTS

CONTENTS

═══

**SLAVE NARRATIVES: A FOLK HISTORY OF SLAVERY
IN THE UNITED STATES, PART 1**

TANKA

SLAVE NARRATIVES: A FOLK HISTORY OF SLAVERY IN THE UNITED STATES, PART 2

TANKA SEQUENCES

FOREWORD

===

Ce Rosenow · FORMER PRESIDENT OF THE
HAIKU SOCIETY OF AMERICA

Crystal Simone Smith is a highly respected, highly talented member of the American Haiku Movement, and a leading figure among African American haiku poets. In *Runagate*, Smith brings her facility with haiku and the related form tanka to a poetic project that breaks new ground with these forms both through their subject matter and through their engagement with other poetic forms and traditions. Drawing on her extensive research at Duke University, Smith crafts a collection of poems that gives voice to enslaved and formerly enslaved persons, contrasting their humanity with the inhumanity of the enslavers. Reviewing materials from Freedom on the Move: A Database of Fugitives from American Slavery and from *Slave Narratives: A Folk History of Slavery in the United States* created the impetus and context for Smith's poems. The resulting haiku sequences, individual tanka, and tanka sequences also function as persona poems, poems of witness, and, in some cases, verse journalism. The resulting collection presents image-centered narratives that bring real people out of historical archives and into first-person, poetic depictions of their experiences, foregrounding the humanity and strength of the enslaved and the brutality of slavery.

The opening section of the book presents haiku sequences written in response to advertisements from slaveholders and jailers. In the ads, slave owners provide descriptions of runaway slaves written from the point of view of the slaveholders and offer rewards for their return. Jailers announce the capture of runaway slaves and ask owners to retrieve them. Left-side pages contain a single ad facing right-side pages presenting one of Smith's haiku sequences written in the persona of the person described in the ad. In this way, Smith participates in what Gwendolyn Brooks termed "verse journalism," as she investigates these events through the creative exploration of what might have been the enslaved person's experiences. The sequences incorporate details from the advertisements while also developing a sense of the fugitives' trauma and commitment to freedom. Although many of the haiku can stand independently, every haiku is more fully realized when read within its sequence. Smith's approach recalls the Japanese *rensaku* tradition, where the meanings of the separate haiku on a topic are enhanced by the full sequence.

In addition to crafting linked verse in the personas of the escaped slaves, Smith also constructs a chronological order of events that adds to the sequences' narrative quality. The combination of the speakers' voices and the chronologies produces an enhanced understanding of the horrors of slavery because there is a greater sense of the fugitives' personhood in contrast to the advertisements' emphasis on humans as property. Poems also depict the dehumanizing effects that slavery had on slaveholders, who were willing to own other humans, separate family members, and torture adults and children.

Using haiku sequences as a lens through which to view African American experiences locates Smith's work in the lineage of poets such as Lenard D. Moore and Sonia Sanchez. Moore's sequences in *Desert Storm* and *A Million Shadows at Noon* consider the military service of African American men and the events of the Million Man March. Sanchez's sequences, especially in *Morning Haiku*, celebrate the achievements and contributions of African American artists, novelists, political activists, and other prominent figures while also elegizing people whose lives were lost due to racist violence. Smith's haiku recall the formal approaches taken by these poets as well. Her more traditional haiku juxtapose two clear images and often incorporate a nature reference, which is consistent with Moore's poems. Smith also experiments with form to better accommodate her project's emphasis on witnessing through the voices and experiences of escaped or freed slaves; therefore, some poems emphasize the human experience beyond what is typically seen in haiku. While not technically *senryu* (haiku-like poems focusing on human affairs and often including humor or commentary), they resonate with many of Sanchez's haiku that are explicitly human-centered. Sanchez's sequences in *Morning Haiku* also refer to actual people and include a reference to them in the title, such as "15 Haiku (for Toni Morrison)." Smith titles her sequences with the name of the person in the advertisement, as with "Peggy," or, if there was uncertainty about the person's actual name, the variations given in the advertisement, as with "Ely or July."

Two tanka sections follow the opening group of linked haiku. Tanka are five-line poems that often present a haiku-like, three-line unit using a short-long-short pattern followed by two longer lines incorporating the speaker's feelings or thoughts. Contemporary English-language tanka, while typically presented in five lines, now follow a variety of line lengths, divisions between units, and subject matters. Smith follows a traditional approach of two units, using both a three-line unit followed by a two-line unit and a two-line unit followed by a three-line unit. Her content sets her tanka apart from other contemporary English-language tanka because once again she draws from historical documents about the experiences of enslaved or formerly enslaved people and writes from their perspective. Her source, *Slave Narratives: A Folk History of Slavery in the United States*, was part of the Federal Writers' Project of the Works Progress Administration and focused on slave narratives from individual states. Smith works specifically with information from North Carolina.

The first tanka section presents poems written in the persona of an actual enslaved person whose story was included in the source material. The poems are printed one per page, allowing for maximum impact. Tanka allow for more narrative description than would be afforded by haiku, yet they are also more focused and condensed than a haiku sequence. The surrounding space on the page keeps the readers' focus on the images and information, giving time to process what is conveyed within the context of the larger collection of poems. The speakers' voices describe the atrocities, emotional and physical, endured by slaves, both adults and children. In several poems, Smith embeds the words of other people so that her speakers are sharing both their thoughts and what they've heard from others. In this way, she creates layers of information and meaning within the compact tanka form.

The section of individual tanka creates a bridge between the beginning and ending sections of sequences. The haiku sequences focus on the time before emancipation and on slaves who escaped to freedom or who escaped and were recaptured. The middle section of the book, while witnessing life under slavery as told in *Slave Narratives*, also addresses experiences after emancipation and during the transition from enslavement to freedom. The final section emphasizes the "former" nature of enslavement endured by the speakers, who, while reflecting on the past, are now free.

The six tanka sequences, or tanka strings, that complete the book provide longer, more developed representations of the personal histories shared in *Slave Narratives: A Folk History of Slavery in the United States*. As in the middle section, each tanka offers more details than would a single haiku; by linking them, Smith constructs an expansive representation of the person's memories. Some of the sequences develop chronologically, while others link together separate recollections. Each emphasizes the emancipated status of the person whose story Smith crafts into poetry. For instance, Smith dedicates the first two sequences to specific persons and refers to their freedom by referring to that status in the subtitle, as in "for former slave Robert Glenn," the format Sanchez uses when subtitling her haiku sequences "for" specific people. The third sequence contains the subtitle "as told by former slave Millie Henry." The final three sequences do not have subtitles but return to the title structure of the haiku sequences that began the collection. In these instances, Smith writes verses within the tanka strings that specifically reference the time when "Yankees finally came," as her speaker says in "Essex Henry." Concluding the book with linked tanka using the speakers' names brings the project full circle. The titles once again rhetorically emphasize the personhood of the people whose stories are shared in the book and are brought forward through their poetic personas crafted by Smith.

Runagate brings a heightened awareness of slavery's human cost. By combining haiku and tanka with other poetic traditions, Smith develops a robust sense of individual people and their lives, including their bravery in the face of extreme cruelty and suffering. Moment by moment and narrative by narrative, she expands the poetic range of haiku and tanka while deepening the reader's understanding of a tragic part of American history and the people who endured it.

PREFATORY NOTE

THE NARRATIVES in *Runagate* reimagine fugitive (or captive) journeys of the enslaved and therefore witness daring acts of human autonomy Tim Tyson calls "to steal one's freedom." The narratives employ the Japanese poetics of haiku, with inclusions of imagery, tension, and nature elements that embody the form. Tanka, the earliest Japanese poetic form (*waka*), is also employed. Both short forms can be composed in stanzas (or sequences) that here extend accounts of fugitivity or survivalism of enslaved figures.

Black poets' engagement in haiku dates to the beginning of the English-language haiku movement. Our approach to the form often diverges to explorations of social politics and culture, shifting beyond the traditional Zen-inspired response to nature. This approach can crescendo into a radical voice calling attention to racism. Of the hundreds of haiku poets who practice and publish in the present day, a mere handful are poets of color. We embody a long-established tradition of poets like Richard Wright, Etheridge Knight, and Lewis Grandison Alexander, whose haiku were first published in *The Messenger* in the 1920s. Lenard D. Moore (b. 1958) is distinguished by having published more haiku than any other black poet.

I was introduced to the form by Moore, and for years my preliminary practice was that of Zen-inspired, nature-induced haiku, the conformal modus of contemporary haiku writers. Undistinctive of Wright and others, a thirst to embrace black identity entered my process. The predisposition to infuse blackness into existent art forms like haiku is not learned or radical. Uncounted realities inform the historical relationship black and white natives have with nature. Whereas black ecopoets align with an appreciation for the natural world, our entanglements contain a legacy of racism manifested over centuries through customs of tree lynchings and forced field labor. Camille Dungy states that the view of nature "is intensified by the black experience of slavery."

My exploration into slavery haiku originated with a slave narrative course I structured years ago. In preparation, I read four narratives that depicted the natural world very differently. For the enslaved, nature was captivity. I found the concept of nature depicted from this angle intriguing, a supposition resisting the singular viewpoint of nature as scenic with the prime motive of calling attention to its pleasurable aspects. The slavery angle affirms the harshness of nature as the milieu of enslavement. This angle was visually curated in the cinematic adaptation of *12 Years a Slave* when Solomon, the enslaved protagonist, lost in the drudgery of fieldwork, pauses to observe the spectacle of a majestic sunset. While seemingly too impressive to ignore, it does not induce pleasure, but frustratingly increases his predicament.

Haiku is an esoteric practice to many contemporaries and critics. Like enslavement, its presence in the larger world today remains rather muted. One of the earliest poetic forms, it is language most distilled, the art of expressing wonderful or powerful meditations with few words. By virtue of its brevity, haiku offers a straightforward way to engage in conversations about slavery. The aesthetics of haiku can increase the intensity of the moment, flooding the reader with sentiment, evoking candid responses. Conjointly intensifying, slave narratives are documented accounts that preserve, collectively, the lives of the enslaved and particular incidents in those lives. Using these testimonies, I began the process of distillation: capturing images and incidents experienced by humans abiding under forced labor, evident in the following haiku:

spring auction
a slave named
Mourning

A notable paradigm of this approach to haiku is Sonia Sanchez's *Haiku and Tanka for Harriet Tubman*. In critique of Sanchez's praise poem for Tubman, Meta Schettler states, "Tubman appears as a shape-shifting giant 'riding thunder' and capable of wrapping herself around the 'legs' and 'eyes' of slavery to inhibit it and reject it." In homage and with affinity, *Runagate* aims to illuminate the experience of the fugitive enslaved.

Such an immersion in the study of institutional slavery is not a practical act, no more so than it was to engage in the phenomenon of freedom when born into captivity. Both are leaps into unknown worlds of unfathomed psychological peril. The reality of the enslaved past requires a form of attention that transcends dimensions of isolation and cruelty to bring the captive and fugitive into view, an avant-garde approach to modern and traditional haiku concerned with one's presence in, and response to, the natural world.

Zen informs haiku, placing strong emphasis on simplicity and presence. The mediative practice often requires a nondualistic approach. Put simply, this translates into "not two": life exists here and now; there is no separation, only one universal essence, one reality. Thus, presence and attention are imperative. By contrast, dualism, philosophically speaking, is the concept of "two." The mind extends beyond the brain as a spirit or soul distinct from the body, one we can imagine surviving the death of the body; it is suggestive of eternal existence. As chattel enslavement is a past event, I was torn in the practice and confessedly still in the silent reckoning of my own ancestral slave lineage. Once, writhed with curiosity, I combed the internet, traced my familiar lineage to the oldest ancestor I could locate. She is listed as the property of a white man, a young woman named Ernestine, born in 1827. Her birth, on the whole unverified but withal not disproven, incited a *haibun* that closes the text. Formal research expanded into the fields of preserved historic plantations, where there was a keen awareness of spirits in the sullen and torrid midsummer air. In response, I generated effective haiku. Notwithstanding, the process with greater yield was that of ekphrasis—writing in response to artifacts, physical documents, and relics of slavery to gain a sense of the bruteness, unremitting surveillance, and psychological toil endured. It was this approach that allowed the "oneness" we strive to achieve in the mediative practice of haiku.

Subsequently, listening to voices of the formerly enslaved whose recorded accounts were archived in the Library of Congress, I gave consideration to the haiku aesthetic, sensation (or senses), to process the terror of tortured beings and the exhilaration of freedom. In these voices, otherwise unheard, was a strict fixation on survivalism. This listening became the framework for my consideration of a time in which *time* was the foremost concern. As haiku practitioners, we believe the poem is a moment left open for individual interpretation or for the reader to finish. Thus, as I encountered Cornell University's Freedom on the Move database of ads generated by slaveholders seeking the capture of runaways, my instinctual thinking was to visualize the journeys of those listed by forename only. The database comprises more than thirty thousand ads that synopsize runaways through marks and scars, acts of insolence cited, or descriptions of individuals' flights.

The actualness of the ads time-marking these freedom performances incited reimaginings of their escapes through images recorded as haiku. Such a process, with the journeys or outcomes of the fugitives unknowable, provoked intense personal depictions that gave an immediacy and matter-of-factness to their plight. As mentioned, this interpretation of the natural world entails a formal separation from Zen principles. While within these poems the reader is able to conjure potential beauty and possibility, the disturbing images are meant to unsettle us and to raise political consciousness, illustrated in the following stanza of the haiku sequence "Clinton":

days I lay resting
bloodied feet
vultures circling

The tanka in *Runagate* respond to documented slave narratives prepared by the Federal Writers' Project between 1936 and 1938. The interviews, I will disclose, often fall under the scrutiny of historians regarding the journalistic accuracy of this sampling of elderly ex-slaves' recollections of childhood incidents. Notwithstanding, the narratives provide candid accounts of emancipation and Reconstruction. Moreover, the interviews give voice to the enslaved, an oral history persistently faulty in or omitted entirely from textbooks. With this expansive source, each interview comprising one or more full pages of text, tanka offered a greater landscape. While brevity is a feature of both haiku and tanka, they differ in structure. Haiku is a three-line poem that captures our awe of nature. Tanka, a five-line poetic form, translates as "short song." The latter form can embrace all of human experience with emotions of love, pity, suffering, loneliness, or death, illustrated in the following tanka:

oh my brother's
cracked-open feet!
we could track him by blood . . .
when the Yankees came
through he got shoes

Presently, five generations removed from slavery, I abide with millions of other descendants as testament to the black intergenerational trauma pervasive in America. New formations of oppression permeate the existence of black lives as modifications of captivity: mass incarceration, housing inequities, educational inequities. Unearthing and chronicling the journey of the enslaved is critical to understanding the effects American slavery has yielded. *Runagate*, through the lenses of escape, recognizes the hopes, loves, and improbable dreams of the enslaved.

PROLOGUE

———

RUNAGATE: WHAT TO THE SLAVE IS THE

SEMIQUINCENTENNIAL?

——WHEN THE WHITE ORTHOPEDIST AT THE TRACK MEET
ASKS ME WHY WE RUN SO WELL

let us run it back // in 2026 we will have been at this occupation two
hundred and fifty black years // though no one merits it // we can take
the heat // recently I hosted a film fest for black college students //
the track runners rose to leave halfway in // when I asked why another
professor said *they have to go into them fields* // there are countless
practices of running from police sirens // the sound of the beast // we
run because in 2016 over one million of us were caged in prisons // in
1926 thousands of us began running north escaping southern torture
and lynchings leaving all that darkness in the distance // in 1826 two
million of us were in chains // we ran barefoot beside rushing creeks
into thickets at night // most of us were captured so we ran again // it
all started around 1776 // Britain's Somerset decision freed us before
America did // colonial generals were forced to make a decision // let
enslaved blacks fight alongside them in exchange for their freedom too
// they refused so thousands of us ran to Nova Scotia to live free under
the British rule colonial slaveholders were escaping.

a fly slamming
against a window—
lush mountain holler

FREEDOM ON THE MOVE

REDISCOVERING THE STORIES OF
SELF-LIBERATING PEOPLE

═══════

HAIKU SEQUENCES

S TOP THE THIEF. A FREE MAN who calls himself, HENRY FIELDS, has stolen from the subscriber living near Salem, Franklin county, a Negro woman name MARIA. The negro man is a low, heavy set fellow, tolerably black, about 5 feet 6 inches high. He has a certificate from Col. Micah Taul, that he is a free man. The girl is of yellow complexion, spare built, about 5 feet high; as I now recollect she has a scar from a burn on one of her cheeks, but not recollected which: she is 18 or 19 years of age. It is thought that they will make for Kentucky, and from there to a free State. I will give **$25** for the apprehension of the girl, and **$25** for the boy, if confined to any Jail so that I can get them. The boy has with him a Fiddle. He stole a Grey Mare from Wm. Devin, near Winchester.

WM. WOODS. August [illegible], 1840
- - w[illegible]

HENRY & MARIA

indigo midnight
I made her the offer
of freedom or heaven

> she took one hand
> in my other
> a gripped fiddle

humid night
our solitude
a paradise

> breaking morning
> I fetch water
> and bread morsels

river crossing
we mask in mud
abandon the mare

> we dwell on
> delivered from under
> the whip

THE CITY GAZETTE   ST. GEORGE'S DORCHESTER,
CHARLESTON, SC, US

Ten Dollars Reward. RUN AWAY from the sub-scriber, a Negro Fellow, named Jemmy, well known as a fisherman and frequently attended the fish market; he is a remarkable tall, robust fellow, aged between 35 and 40: had on when he went off a blue jacket, trowsers and a sailor's cap Whoever lodges him in the Work-House, or brings him to No. 56, Bay, shall receive the above reward.

Francis Breen. April 4.

JEMMY

fiery dusk
he left my flesh
in pieces

red moon
my spirit too daring
for Massa

northward
rebel as ever
I trod the soil

trampling free
with the trout
I hooked

the river's
chattering run
a moonlit map

near dawn
my back aching
in barn warmth

$5 REWARD.—Ran away, a negro woman named LUCY, the property of the subscriber. She is black and has a stiff finger on her left hand. The above reward will be paid to whoever will bring the said slave to the subscriber's residence, or lodge her in any jail in this city.

CHAS. MEYEIL, a9 corner of Circus
and Julia sts.

LUCY

lifetime of toil
I pass through
fire and water

broken promises
old mistress sold me

her stroke paralysis
the bill of sale
signed with a cross

neighboring plantation
I wander far away

the old cemetery
souls gone from evil
days to come

in the distance
field song

THE CITY GAZETTE ST. GEORGE'S DORCHESTER,
CHARLESTON, SC, US 06/07/1797

TAKEN up, and brought to the Work-House, a
NEGRO BOY, who says his name is ASKO, or
GLASGOW; that he belongs to Mr. FULLER, living about
7 miles from town; Guinea born, has a scar on his fore-
head apparently done with a knife, very much marked on
his back with a whip, speaks bad English, about 10 years
of age, 4 feet 2 Vi inches high.

A. SEIXAS, Master. June 7.

ASKO OR GLASGOW

back marked
by the whip's lick
worn trekked path

swallowed up
walking the earth

marshlands
sunken in the coolness
blistered heels

meadowland
no harborage in view

asleep under stars
all the sounds
in the silence

behold, he stood
over me a ghost

$50 REWARD—Absconded from the subscriber, on the 20th May, 1845, the Negro Man CLINTON, about 30 years old, six feet high, reddish complexion, speaks English and a little French. He has a scar on the right foot, and another on the left toe. This boy ran away once before and was caught near Vicksburg, Miss. The said reward will be given for his apprehension and delivery in one of the jails of this State, or to the subscriber.

LUCIEN LABRANCHE, je17 15t Parish
of Jefferson.

CLINTON

cotton near
in full bloom
I ran madly

    choosing my
    own death field—
    the quiet thicket

days I lay resting
bloodied feet
vultures circling

    light lifts
    edge of the pond
    a tolerable step

on the move—
the blessing
of morning fog

E SCAPED by breaking the Jail of the Parish o Jeffer-
son, on the night of Tuesday 11th inst, an American
Negro named Jack, aged about 45 years; who has lost
his toes. Also, a French negro named Paul, aged about
27 years, with large eyes and prominent features. He says
that he belongs to madam Bourgeois.

GEORGE DE PASSAU, Sheriff,
Parish of Jefferson, March 14 1828.

JACK (AND PAUL)

born a slave
I believed I had
no soul

this one life
I would not
die a slave

supper hour
I tied overseer to
the whipping post

evening heat
I put him under
the lash and ran

caught and maimed
nor would I die
in the jail cell

we heard faint
sounds of revel
in the lit streets

like birds to song
thereabouts
we wished to be

ONE HUNDRED DOLLARS REWARD. RUNAWAY or was STOLEN on 6th July last. A YELLOW BOY by the name of PETER about fifteen or sixteen years old, heavy made with clumsy feet, otherwise he is hard to detect, being very white with blue or yellowish eyes, straight fair hair, very intelligent when spoken to; took with him a new pair of white janes pantaloons and a short coat, a pair of neat high quartered pin bottomed shoes, new with buckskin strings in them, a new hat, and other articles of clothes to tedious to mention.

PETER

burning bright
the sun reddened
my fair skin

      the fire of it
      cruel as the whip's . . .
      I stole a straw hat

begged to pick
seeds from the cotton
under the sycamore

      for it all
      I was flogged
      as he recited scripture

I could not stay
under a brutal master
who was a good preacher

B rought to Jail, IN Decatur, DeKalb county, Georgia
on the 16th of February, a negro man by the name of
DAVE, about 30 years of age, chunky built, of dark com-
plexion, who says that he belongs to Dr. George Rastor,
of Baker county, and that he left home in July last — The
owner is requested to come forward and prove property,
pay expenses and take him away.

SIMEON WILLIAMS, Jailer. February
16th, 1842.

DAVE

long gone
the glittering chains
of tyrannical masters

sold four times
now this new master's
softened heart

labor with ease
hardy suppers in
indigo fields

I wandered
into the groves
far and lost

captured by patrol
a promise made
to return me home

Five Dollars Reward WILL be paid for apprehending and lodging in the Work-House, a MULATTO WENCH, named GRACE. She has for some time past lived in an out building belonging to Mrs. Yates, on White Point; but because she has lately been offered to be hired out by the month, herself to have nothing to do with her wages, she has absconded. She is therefore considered as a run-away. And, besides the above Reward, Five Dollars will be paid on proof of her being hired by any one without a Ticket from me, from this day, or harboured and entertained in the smallest degree. Her husband is a tall Mulatto Fellow, named TOM, a fisherman, belonging to Mrs. Johnston, formerly Mrs. John Dewees.

Henry Gray. St. James's, Goose Creek,
Aug. 4.

GRACE (AND TOM)

My lover's promise
for us to take the river
to our freedom

one day when whipped
he asked Master to pray

he was thrown
on the stagecoach
took off and sold

each new harvest no suffering
like our mutual suffering

Now I move free
between plantations—
if I run, he'll follow

L EFT the Plantation of the Subscriber in Wilkinson County, the 5th of March last, my negro woman Mariah Frances, about 18 years old of light complexion. Having purchased said negro from Mrs. M. E. Blount of Milledgeville, GA, it may be that she is lurking about that place, or her Plantation in Washington County. I will pay **Twenty-Five dollars** for the delivery of the girl to me, or in any jail so that I can get her. If said negro is harbored by any white person, I will pay One Hundred Dollars for evidence to convict.

T.C. WHITEHURSET, Gordon, Ga.
May 20, 1839.

MARIAH FRANCES

morning chores
my downcast face
met at every turn

his footsteps,
his foul words
whispered

sundown fields
he trod my heels
. . . this new tomb

his shadow
cast over me
brute tormentor

overpowered
I shivered
with disgust

I turned my face
to the North Star
homebound

FIVE DOLLARS REWARD. (Peggy Ran away.) The Wench PEGGY absented herself from her master three days ago. She is about 40 years of age; may change her clothing, having plenty; she was formerly the property of Mary G. Rivers; has a husband named Frank at Col. Magwood's. She is about 5 feet high, dresses and looks decent, not very black. The above Reward will be paid to anyone who will lodge her at the Work House; and persons found harboring her will be prosecuted to the rigor of the law. Apply at this office. th November 2

1/13/1825

PEGGY

Mistress Mary's
old handspun dresses
a blessing and curse

my new ol' master
resolved to possess
every part of me

not allowed to sit down
while I ate my meals

to rest my weary limbs
after hauling wood
all day for hearths

moonless nights
too tired to fight
off his violations

new dewy morning
his trek to my empty cot

only God see'st me
dizzy on a winding
autumn path

$10 REWARD—Ran away on the 6th inst. the black boy JOHN or JOHN BULL, aged about 30 years, five feet four inches in height, very stout built, round face, badly marked by small pox, and a scar produced from an attempt to cut his throat. The said boy was bought some nine months since from —— Miller, and is supposed to be loitering about the Old Basin or Lake end of the Railroad. The above reward will be paid to anyone who will produce him to me or lodge him in any jail so that I may get him. jy28-1m GEO. G. KIRK, Race st.

08/08/1846

JOHN BULL

like many slaves
I did not know
how to run away

I would run deep
into the woods
for days then return

I cried for the giver
of all good to deliver
me from bondage

so mangled by the lash
I once sought my own
grave from Master

all law being
in his favor he knew
no night or Sunday

when he slept
I stole hours to sleep—
resolved to leave

I would meet him
only once again
at the judgment seat

TWO HUNDRED DOLLARS REWARD Look out for AUSTIN, who was supposed to have been burned on the steamer Charles Belcher, but who, I now have reason to believe, escaped under cover of that disaster. Austin was purchased by me from Sertain & Lumpkin, of Huntsville, Ala., and raised by John Connelly of the same place. He is a likely yellow boy about 21 years of age, weighing about 140 pounds; is a good cook, barber and carriage driver, and has I believe a scar on his left cheek. He is quite sprightly [illegible] has a good address. I suppose he is either lurking about this city or is making his way to Huntsville or some free State. I will give this reward for his delivery to Messrs. Hemmingway & Friedlander, of this city, or to myself in Holmes county, Miss. MORGAN MCAFEE ap7 Huntsville (Ala.) Democrat please copy one month, and forward account to Hemmingway, Friedlander & co., New Orleans.

08/08/1854

AUSTIN

scorched flesh
upon my legs and feet
I crept in wilderness

escaping patrol
I climbed the peak
of a magnolia tree

old hounds
taken up with a rabbit—
this deep hush

patrollers' rifles
glistened by the light
of the moon

morning twilight
wet with dew
and hungry

I board a boat
stow myself away
among the bales

$10 REWARD Ranaway from the Subscriber in July last, his servant ELY, commonly calls himself JULY. A description is needless, as he is well known, belonging to the Pilot Boat Comfort. Since her loss, he was hired to Capt. Halwells of the Pucket Boat, and afterwards had a badge to work on the wharves generally, was also hired by Mr. [illegible] Patton, to work on the Steamboat wharf. He has been all the Summer fishing and lorking about the Islands and in the City. He is at present somewhere about the market selling Oysters. If any information can be given of his being harbored by white persons, a liberal reward will be given Nov 30 3

RICHARD CLARK
12/03/1836

ELY OR JULY

lost in the chaos
of a sea storm
I found myself alone

both white and black
faces scattering to shelter

wild wind gusts
and rising waters
night as black as ink

I sank in the water
leaving only my nose
and mouth above

there I remained
through the storm

with only stars
strewn overhead
I drifted far away

TWENTY DOLLARS REWARD SHALL be promptly paid to any person, who will take up and secure (so that I get him) my negro man Robbin, ran off on the 7th April last, without the least provocation, having never received a lick either from me or anyone under me. Robbin is about 35 years of age, is likely and of just stature and proportion, he is somewhat Tawney and has a scar on his left eye-brow said to have been made by a whip, which causes the eye-lid to hang a little lower than the other. His back is smartly cut by former owners, he is brisk in his movements, is handy, very plausible and knows how to spay hogs. I purchased Robbin of John King of this county, about 12 months ago, who had him of one Russell of Johnston county. It is probable Robbin is now lurking his old range between Kings, Russell's and Mr. James Hinton's where he has a wife, or has gone lower down toward Newbern.

JNO.[John] W. CHARLES.
Wake County, June 25, 1821.

ROBBIN

nearly wild
with longing
for my wife

I lowly begged
my new master
for one last visitation

his word was law
I was chained to a post
like a horse

I remained hitched
until cool shade
became starlit night

I broke the chain
ran through fields
past droves of hogs

we made silent love
under bell-shaped
blossoms

Ten Dollars Reward. RUN AWAY from the Sub-scriber, in Edgecomb County, on Friday the 9th instant, about 13 miles above Tarborough, 4 miles south of Tar River, my NEGRO FELLOW SAM. He is about forty years old, very black, and of tolerable size. One of his upper fore teeth split, which makes them rather stand apart. He took with him a new homespun shirt and trowsers, two blankets, and sundry other cloaths not recollected. He pretend[s] to be a doctor, and it is probable he may attempt to pass for a free man. I know not what course he may go. I will give the above reward, if delivered to me, or confined in any jail, so that I get him again.

JANE WILLIAMS.
July 17. 3t

SAM

when Mistress's fever
would not break
I fetched wild roots

dressed her bed
and spooned her
the remedy tea

nearing death
she promised my freedom
in exchange for living

fever released—
to her promise
she laid no claim

the laws of slavery
making all masters
human demons

I escaped at night
prayers answered—
light of a Negro cabin

a woman gave me
water and bread
in the name of a disciple

FIFTY DOLLARS REWARD. RUNAWAY FROM THE UNDERSIGNED ON THE 25th December, a negro boy named ANDERSON, about twenty-five years old, perfectly black—heavy set, and weight from 175 to 190 pounds when he left.—He has been hand-cuffed. Said by[sic] is supposed to have been raised by Mr. Lewis, of Sampson county, N. C.—When he left he had on a blue jacket and white pants, very ragged; has good teeth and speaks freely. I bought him of Mr. L. P. Robinson, of Augusta, Ga., on the 15th instant, and was on my way to Richmond Va., and had to lay over in Raleigh on account of not being able to get passage. I was camped by the side of the Railroad track. He left about dark. I will pay the above reward to any person who will deliver said boy to any jail for safe-keeping so that I can get him. Any information will be thankfully received.

SOLOMON COHEN, Care John B.
Davis, Richmond, Va. Dec 26-1w
12/26/1862

ANDERSON

winter morning—
the auction block's
gathered crowd

the auctioneer's
echoed cries for bids

our family of four
sold off to purchasers
separated forevermore

this lone journey
I memorized curves
of the river bend

almost Christmas
I count the leafless trees

no matter the lash
I'll return my arms—
one final goodbye

50 DOLLARS REWARD. ABSCONDED from the subscriber on the 3rd of August last, a negro girl named EMILY, about 18 or 20 years of age, of common height, slender form, and rather light complexion. She took with her a variety of clothing, among which was a calico frock and another of striped domestick cloth. Emily has relations in Newbern, among the slavery of Isaac Taylor, Esq.[Esquire] and also on Core Creek, in Craven County, and is probably concealed in the neighborhood of one those places. The above reward will be given for apprehension and delivery to me, or for her confinement in any jail so that I get her, besides the reimbursement of any reasonable expense that may be incurred in her apprehension.

B. COLEMAN, Elm Grove,
Dec. 18th, 1836.

EMILY

journeying homeward
I traveled in darkness
by day thick woodlands

three weeks to reach
woods near my kinfolk—
Mammy, Papa, brother

in a hollow I lived
a den hidden
under the house

they supplied all
my provisions—
visited me careful

tied their feet
in bundles of rags
to leave no tracks

FORTY DOLLARS REWARD. A reward of Forty Dollars will be given to any one who will apprehend and secure in the Wilmington jail the following Negro Women: Harriet, Bella, Elsey and Milly. HARRIET is a tall thin wench of a yellowish complexion about thirty two or thirty three years of age, well known in Wilmington, where her parents are and supposed to be harbored in the neighborhood of Town Creek Bridge. BELLA a short wench—her complexion similar to that of Harriet's, who I have reason to believe is secreted in town. ELSEY is also a short wench, her complexion deeper than either of the others, has remarkable white teeth and speaks quick—She is supposed to be frequently in town and at Mr. George Mackenzie's plantation (Lilliput) where she has a husband—she is about twenty-five years of age. MILLY is a slender wench of the common height, her complexion very much of the mulatto; she is about three and twenty years of age and may be found either in town or at Mr. George MacKenzie's plantation. Forty dollars will be given for their delivery in the Wilmington jail or ten for either of them.

WILLIAM H. MACKENZIE.
April 1. 06/19/1810

HARRIET, BELLA, ELSEY, AND MILLY

we witnessed
a spent slave
large with child

give offense
in the field
to the overseer

made to lie down
over a hole
dug to receive her

flogged so severe
with the whip
labor was brought on

purple sundown
the child was born
in the field

we gathered
in the valley
wept for her

concluded to claim
our weary bodies
as our own

SLAVE NARRATIVES

A FOLK HISTORY OF SLAVERY IN
THE UNITED STATES, PART I

———

TANKA

hard worked days
& half food rations—
by night my daddy
would hunt down
coons and possums

one pair of shoes
worn out & tied up
with strings—
where we walked we left
bird-like tracks

we spent nights
in our plank houses
cooked suppers and slept . . .
if the firewood was out
we worked Sundays too

for breaking dishes
and being slow
I was public whipped
grove onlookers silent
as the graveyard

oh my brother's
cracked-open feet!
we could track him by blood . . .
when the Yankees came
through he got shoes

dead slave woman
in a wagon carried off
to a field song . . .
Oh come! Let us go
where pleasure never dies

the worst sales—
mamas from children
heaps of groans and hollers
we heard the chains
her whole body rocked

hit in the head
a hand that weighed
a hundred pounds
I didn't work for
seven days and nights

our mama cooked
in the great house
snuck us pies & cookies
we couldn't be happy
scared of being sold

Mistress Mary was kind
barn dances & holidays
she had a heap of beehives
Mama had to tell those
bees when she died

I was awakened
dressed in the dark . . .
down the silent path
bushes slapping my legs
wind in the trees

day the Yankees came
Master walked & cussed—
they took all my Niggers
I walked clean to Raleigh
to find out if I was free

I had sixteen children
twelve were sold away
eighty-one years old
I can still outwork
all my daughters

Smithfield slave market
purchaser of forty slaves
chained them behind
his cart to walk or trot
the way to Richmond

allowed no pleasures
when we sang
we turned a pot
down at the door
to catch the noise

Master made me go
with him to war
to fight the Yankees
he on the big horse
I on the stubborn mule

we worked winter
from sun to sun
ate frozen bread
if we made a fire
overseer put it out

Christmas Eve
Daddy told me
I was a free man
and that was all
he had to give me

SLAVE NARRATIVES

A FOLK HISTORY OF SLAVERY IN

THE UNITED STATES, PART 2

━━━━━━

TANKA SEQUENCES

AIN'T YOU MY CHILD

As a boy I was sold
Mother was told
under the whip's threat
not to cry out
when they took me

        —FOR FORMER SLAVE
        ROBERT GLENN

she heard through
the grapevine telegraph
I was off to Kentucky
and asked permission
to come say goodbye

Master ordered two
slave girls to oversee
said if I escaped they'd
be whipped every day
until I was caught

when parting came
I burst out crying
so weak I couldn't walk
they carried me off
held up by each arm

new Master's son
loved me & we played
school in secret
only the slaves knew
I could write & read

the war ended, Master
said I was as free
as he was but I stayed
Yankees ordered him
to pay and board me

slow to freedom
I fished & hunted
at night I drew
castles in the air &
made plan after plan

I went to Illinois
to look for work
haunted in dreams
and waking hours
I vowed to see Mama

I traveled south
under a fictitious name—
at her door I shook
her worn hand
& held it too long

unknown to her
I lingered in the room . . .
suspicious she whispered
Ain't you my child?
we wept & wept

AFTER THE STARS FELL

One of the most spectacular
meteor showers on record,
visible over North America, 1833

—FOR FORMER SLAVE
SARAH GUDGER

As we played after supper
Mama summoned us
& said, *look up at the sky*
bless your life, honey
stars were falling like rain

night was bright as day
Mama grew scared,
said fallen stars meant
someone was leaving
not long after she was sold

I was left alone
to care for myself
I worked sun to sun
plowing, hoeing, humming
in the boiling sun

I never slept in a bed
until freedom came
just in a pile of rags
in a corner hardly enough
to keep me warm

we had no doctors
if you got sick
they gathered herb roots
from the woods
to bring you back

I'd lie awake till
everyone fell asleep
walk barefoot in the snow
to my aunt's house
for a slice of meat

one day Mama's master
came to tell me she died
I went to my mistress
for permission to see her
before they put her away

my mistress looked
at me with mean eyes
told me to get back
to work before she
whipped me good!

I went back to my work
wringing my hands with
tears down my face
weeks later my mistress
got terrible sick and died

when the Yankees came
Master said we was free . . .
in all my life I never been sick,
took doctor's medicine
only once after freedom

CONFEDERATE LIEUTENANT
ROBERT WALSH

caught when his horse tired
he fell off and stumbled—
to the redheaded general
he confessed his name
Robert Walsh

—AS TOLD BY
FORMER SLAVE
MILLIE HENRY

confessed why he shot
at the General's men—
'cause he hates Yankees
laughs and wishes they
were dead in a pile

General ordered him carried
out of sight of the women
carried off to be killed
he went into a laughing fit
as they strung him up

they hung him in Lovejoy grove
buried him under the tree
then in a cemetery grave
covered in wildflowers
and young ladies' tears

JOE HIGH

too young to work
in the cotton fields
I stayed quiet, kept
chickens out the garden
& flies from the table

my mother brought me
hot potlikker and bread
I can't remember one word
my mother ever said
or spoke to me

we children ate beans
out of one bowl
with mussel shells
in the white church we sat
in a corner to ourselves

after the war I studied
so I could learn to read
hymns and songs
I kept an old slave book
recorded ages & deaths

SARAH ANNE GREEN

I had my pappy's eyes
blue like Master Billy's
my ol' master
was pappy's master
and his pappy too

every Christmas Master
gave us a big time
called us to the big house
gave us bags of candy
and sugar plums

Who wants eggnog?
if we wanted dram
we held up our hands
he said I was too young
then gave me a glass

good foamy eggnog
mixed with rich cream
Master served it himself
kept his daughters busy
filling up the glass bowl

when the Yankees come
I loved their blue coats
with shiny brass buttons
I followed them round
begging for the buttons

I followed the Yankees
down the road until
one gave me his button
said he'd never seen blue eyes
in a black face before

ESSEX HENRY

we were spirited
wouldn't be whipped
my uncle was sold off for it
my grandmother would
not be whipped

overseer called Master
who kicked in her stomach
carried to the sick cabin
she died three days later
nothing done for her

the coffin was carried
by horses on a wagon
with all the slaves
following and singing
swing low sweet chariot.

Master & the white folks
refused to come to the grave
so we were free to sing
we could have no religion
on our plantation

Master's brother & uncle
would come visiting
they loved slave suffering
like they loved brandy
they'd whip slaves all day

the war lasted & lasted
Yankees finally came riding
Master flew the coop
left barrels of brandy
we stayed and drank it

EPILOGUE

———

HAIBUN FOR ANCESTOR ERNESTINE
TURNER (B. 1827)

—— IN DISCOVERY AND MEMORY

A damp darkness fell upon me as I sat lost in a day of finding ancestors. From sunup, I combed through slavery records on the internet. Finally, there she was, suspended in a database tree where the races blended and our dark skin began. She is not locatable in the census. She is the grandmother of my great-great-grandfather and the property of a white man. He is listed as the father of her six children. She is listed by first name only with a birth year, here where my family tree changes shade, consentingly or not.

evening downpour
a screech owl
switches trees

ACKNOWLEDGMENTS

I EXTEND ABIDING GRATITUDE to Tsitsi Jaji and Adriane Lentz-Smith for so generously welcoming me to Duke University in the role of research fellow, and to the Andrew W. Mellon Foundation–funded Humanities Unbounded, an initiative that afforded me the benefits of financial support, permitted travel, and dedicated time to write.

Equal gratitude to my fellow scholars and faculty at Saint Augustine's University for your support, collaborations, and encouragement.

To the early supporters of this book, Sheila Smith McKoy, Tim Tyson, Michael Dylan Welch, Ce Rosenow, and members of the Carolina African American Writers Collective: I am grateful to you and for you.

To Sparks and Wiry Cries and Martha Guth for the extraordinary song-set project that transformed many of these poems to *Songs in Flight*, and to Grammy-nominated composer Shawn E. Okpebholo, soprano Karen Slack, countertenor Reginald Mobley, baritone Will Liverman, and instrumentalist Rhiannon Giddens: I bow to you. (The premiere *of Songs in Flight* at the Metropolitan Museum of Art in New York is available via YouTube.)

I need to sing praise of Cornell University's Freedom on the Move: A Database of Fugitives from American Slavery, a compelling source that inspired the haiku sequences and launched this journey.

Last, I extend gratitude to the journal *Frogpond* for previously publishing "For Ancestor Ernestine Turner (b. 1827)," "Mariah Frances," and "Jemmy" in "Cultural Journeys: An Interview with Crystal Simone Smith." Interview by Tom Sacramona. *Frogpond Journal* 45, no. 2 (2022): 65.

FREEDOM ON THE MOVE

═══

A Note

The fugitive ads in the Freedom on the Move database are important inclusions to this text. They serve not only as muse for the poems, but also as critical documentation of the atrocities of chattel slavery, underscoring a perpetual flight response by captives to the violence of human commodification. Historian Loren Schweninger's *Counting the Costs: Southern Planters and the Problem of Runaway Slaves, 1790–1860* demystifies economic practices routinely employed by planters to capture runaways.

While we have no definitive way to know how many enslaved laborers ran away, it appears very few slave owners were immune to the phenomenon. Schweninger mentions New Orleans physician Samuel Cartwright, who coined the term *drapetomania* for a purported mental disease causing the enslaved to run away. Cartwright offered the cure of providing slaves adequate food and housing; if the disease persisted, owners should whip the afflicted until they fell into a submissive state. Such pseudoscience serves today as one of the leading examples of scientific racism. Schweninger contends that most slaves ran away to escape cruel treatment by owners or to rejoin family or partners they were separated from in slave auctions and sales.

In most of the ads I encountered, the average reward offered ranged from $10 to $30. According to Schweninger, "A comparison of average rewards with average slave prices reveals that generally owners offered five percent or less of the value of the runaway as a reward." He also notes that costs could mount for slaves who possessed special skills and were "especially intelligent, or industrious." Case in point: Austin is described in one ad as a cook, barber, and driver, suggesting the possible role of a personal assistant rather than a field hand. The hefty $200 reward is also suggestive of information Austin could possess that might be damaging if revealed. Schweninger explains that in most cases, especially for large planters, the costs associated with runaways were written off as a business expense.

I also observed a trend of higher rewards for younger slaves and lower rewards for women. The range likely tracks the life expectancy of a slave, which most research findings place at about thirty-five years, a reflection of harsh labor conditions. Because of strength advantages, men were considered more valuable workers than women; thus higher rewards were offered for men. Despite the frequent abscondings, most runaway slaves were captured by slave catchers, returned, and disciplined within fifteen days.

These ads reveal a hard history of economic exploitation that many Americans have been sheltered from within our educational systems. Primary sources like Freedom on the Move (https://freedomonthemove.org/) provide us with an understanding of the pivotal role chattel slavery played in the development of our country.

www.ingramcontent.com/pod-product-compliance
Lightning Source LLC
Chambersburg PA
CBHW031932120525
26572CB00023B/254